# CHINA
# Beautiful Landscapes

 CHINA INTERCONTINENTAL PRESS

# ‖ Preface

China is a country located in East Asia to the west of the Pacific Ocean in the eastern hemisphere. With a vast territory accounting for 9.6 million square kilometers, the total land area of China takes up 1/15 of the total land area of the globe and 1/4 of that of Asia. It is equal in size to the entire continent of Europe and is the third largest country in the world after Russia and Canada. China's land borders with other countries staggering 20,000 kilometers. In all China has borders with 14 neighboring countries: D.P.R. Korea in the east, Russia and Mongolia in the northeast and north, Kazakhstan, Kyrgyzstan, Tajikistan, Afghanistan, and Pakistan in the west, and India, Nepal, Bhutan, Myanmar, Laos, and Vietnam in the southwest and south. Chinese ocean territory is as large as 3 million square kilometers, and is one of the largest in the world. The neighboring oceans, including the Bohai Sea, the Yellow Sea, the East China Sea and the South China Sea, join the Pacific Ocean from north to south. The continental coastline extends for more than 18,000 kilometers, along which many islands, large or small, are scattered. In all there are over 6,500 such islands each with an area of more than 500 square meters, among which Taiwan is the largest followed by Hainan Island. Across the seas China faces South Korea, Japan, the Philippines, Brunei, Malaysia and Indonesia.

The distance from the northernmost to the southernmost parts of China is 5,200 kilometers. This immense latitudinal area covers a great number of climates, environments and altitudes. It is one of very few countries with such a large variety of climatic zones within its borders. From Heilongjiang Province in the north to the south, there are in total five climatic zones: a cold temperate zone, a mesothermal zone, a warm temperate zone, a subtropical zone and a tropical zone. Zengmu Ansha, the southernmost point in China, is very close to being in the equatorial climatic zone. On the high plateaus is found an extensive, cold climatic zone. Most of China is located within the temperate, warm temperate and subtropical zones. In general, the lands of China provide a favorable climatic location for habitation with most areas enjoying four distinct seasons. In some parts of China, one can also find a monsoon climate. From September to the following April, dry and cold winter monsoon winds sweep from Siberia and the Mongolian Plateau. The weather is cold and dry but there is a great difference in temperature between the north and the south. From April to the following September, warm and humid summer monsoons sweep from the ocean. The whole country is characterized by high temperatures and considerable precipitation, with little temperature difference between the north and the south. However, the precipitation differs considerably across different regions from south to north and from east to west. In general, the distribution of annual precipitation becomes less as one moves from the southeastern coast to the northwestern hinterland. The coastal areas of the southeast have an average annual precipitation of more 1,600 mm while the vast region of the northwest has an annual precipitation of less than 50 mm.

The terrain of China slopes from west to east. The terrain in the west is mostly mountainous, with many plateaus and basins, among which the famous Qinghai-Tibet Plateau is known as "Roof of the World". The terrain in the east features mostly plains and hills, which become gradually lower as one moves eastward from the Qinghai-Tibet Plateau in the north. The west to east sloping terrain causes the major rivers of China to flow into the sea.

China has a wide variety of topographies. There are large criss-crossing mountain ranges, enormous plateaus, endless plains, and basins surrounded by mountains and hills. China is a mountainous country, in which mountainous areas account for some 70 percent of its total land area. Mountainous areas constitute the topographical backbone of the Chinese hinterland, scattered amongst which are plateaus, plains and basins of different shapes and sizes. Most mountain ranges extend from east to west or from northeast to southwest but a small number of mountain ranges run from south to north or from northwest to southeast.

China is characterized by multiple climates and complex topographies. It is home to numerous famous mountains and large rivers. Some of the natural beauty of the Chinese landscape is among the most spectacular on earth.

The land of China abounds in mountainous and water landscapes. The mountainous landscapes include granite topography of towering mountain peaks and groups of standing stone columns, such as Mt. Qianshan in Liaoning, Mt. Huangshan in Anhui, Mt. Taishan in Shandong, Mt. Huashan in Shaanxi, and Mt. Helanshan in Ningxia;

imposing and magnificent metamorphic topography seen in such mountains as Mt. Songshan, Mt. Lushan in Jiangxi and Mt. Wutaishan in Shanxi; sandstone peaks unique to China, such as the enormous Wulingyuan scenery zone in Hunan Province, which extends for hundreds of kilometers of strange mountain and rock formations that form what appears a spectacular natural palace; and lastly unique volcanic lava formations found all over the country. Danxia formations, which are found in more than 350 places, are important geological resources and tourist attractions. The most famous consist of over 200 strange mountains and peaks. The most typical and largest of China's Danxia formations include Mt. Danxiashan in Guangdong, Mt. Wuyishan in Fujian, Mt. Maijishan in Gansu and Mt. Qingchengshan in Sichuan. The unique Yadan formation is to be found in Lop Nor in Xinjiang, Wolho Ghost Town and the Cold Lake and Tsaidam Basin in Qinghai. Karst peaks are beautiful and magnificent. Magnificent karst caves are found mainly in Guangxi, Guizhou and eastern Yunnan. The most famous caves are found in the Guilin and Yangshuo areas of Guangxi, where the mountains and hills are mostly circular or conical in shape as if huge mushrooms are rising from underground. As anyone with a basic knowledge of geology is aware, there are no mountains without caves. Glaciers and mountaineering locations are mostly found on the Qinghai-Tibet Plateau. Landscapes carved by wind and sand are mainly located in the northwestern regions.

China possesses a great number of rivers and lakes. There are more than 2,000 rivers in China. The Yangtze River is the largest of the rivers in China and one of the longest rivers in the world. Along the river is to be found scenery of unrivalled natural beauty, the most famously, magnificent and mysterious Three Gorges. The Yellow River is the second longest river in China, and is often called the mother river of the Chinese nation. Along the Yellow River is also to be found some amazing natural scenery. The most beautiful river in China is probably the Lijiang River, which is known by many as the "50-Kilometer Gallery", such is the beauty of the landscapes along its banks. The Huangguoshu Falls, located in southwest Guizhou Province, is the largest waterfall in China and one of the most wonderful waterfalls in all the world. In China, the rivers, valleys, lakes, springs, waterfalls and seashores form landscapes whose beauty has taken the breath away and inspired the awe and wonder of countless generations lucky enough to gaze upon them.

Many of the natural landscapes of China are among the great jewels of the world. The Huanglong and Jiuzaigou scenic areas in Sichuan, the Wulingyuan area in Hunan, and the "Three Parallel Rivers" in Qinghai are officially listed as among the greatest and most beautiful of natural heritages in the world and have all been put under special protection. Mt. Huangshan in Anhui, Mt. Taishan in Shandong, Mt. Wuyishan in Fujian and Mt. Emeishan (Leshan Buddha Statue) of Sichuan are listed as natural and cultural heritages subject to special protection. China's vast territory includes landscapes of enormous variety from the east to the south to the west and to the north. Beautiful, green fertile land stretches away to area south of the Yangtze River, loess plateaus and deserts characterize the northwest, freezing winter landscapes of ice and snow adorn Heilongjiang Province and lush tropical forests dominate Hainan Province, to say nothing of the vast and beautiful Qinghai-Tibet Plateau which consists of icy peaks, snow-capped mountains, and sky-blue lakes and valleys.

According to its different characteristics in terms of topography and culture, China can be divided into four main areas---the northern area, the southern area, the northwestern area and the Qinghai-Tibet area.

# || Contents

Northern Area

The northern area includes the three northeastern provinces of Heilongjiang, Jilin and Liaoning as well as the five provinces downstream of the Yellow River (Hebei, Shandong, Henan, Shanxi and Shaanxi), in addition to the two municipalities of Beijing and Tianjin.

In the northern area, the three northeastern provinces boast advantageous geographic and natural conditions. This area is surrounded from the west, north and east by the Heilongjiang River and the Lesser Hing'an Mountains to the north and the Mt. Changbai-shan and the Yalujiang River to the east. In the middle is the Northeastern Plain, the largest plain with the richest soil in China. The Northeastern Plain has four distinct seasons. Its winter is long and cold with only a short frost-free period while the summers are cool and pleasant. It is a good place to escape the extreme heat of summer in other regions. In the mountainous areas of the northeast are found extensive forested areas. The Greater Hing'an mountain range is dominated by large virgin forests, mainly larch trees. The Changbaishan Mountain Nature Reserve, which has been approved by the UN's "Man and Biosphere" nature protection network, contains a mixture of conifer and Chinese pine forest and broad-leaf deciduous forest. In the forest areas of the northeast are to be found numerous examples of stunning natural scenery throughout the four seasons. One can see lush, green trees in spring, flower-dappled mountains and sparkling streams in summer, cool, pleasant, fresh air and multicolored leaves in autumn and purest snowdrifts in winter. The winter of the northeast is uniquely harsh. The snow and ice of Harbin and the rime of Jilin are spectacular sights to see and unique to the northeast. Wuda Lianchi and the volcanic rock formations of the Mt. Changbaishan are also well known beauty spots in the northeast. Moreover, there are also large wetland areas.

The five provinces downstream of the Yellow River together constitute most of the North China Plain and the Loess Plateau. The Mt. Taihangshan separate the North China Plain from the Loess Plateau. This is the birthplace of Huanghe Culture, a most famous representative Chinese civilization. The Yellow River, the very lifeblood of this region, is the second largest river in China. It flows in the shape of "几" and winds slowly towards the sea. In Shanxi Province it narrows to pass through high mountains on both sides and forms the Hukou Falls, one of the great wonders of the Yellow River due to its violent water flow. The Yellow River runs through flourishing pastures, the magnificent Loess Plateau and the vast North China Plain. The Loess Plateau is large in both area and soil thickness. It covers more than 300,000 square kilometers, with the maximum soil thickness reaching between one and two hundred meters. Its breadth and wildness form a rich topography unique in all the world. The virgin environment of the Loess Plateau includes both forest and grassland. Grasslands grow in great profusion while small areas of forest are found in places of lower altitude. After thousands of years' human activity, the virgin grasslands have been all but destroyed. The loess is rich in calcium carbonate, which is hard when dry but becomes muddy when wet. It flows away with the waters of the Yellow River and consequently the Loess Plateau has experienced serious water loss and soil erosion. This phenomenon has been continuing for an extremely long period of time. According to geologists, it may take thousands of years at least. The middle reaches of the Yellow River run through the Loess Plateau, where large amount of loess is taken into the river. Thus the river becomes a true "yellow river". In areas midstream and downstream of the Yellow River, the weather is most pleasant. It is not too cold in winter and not too hot in summer. The natural scenery alters and transforms with the changing seasons.

In the northern area there are many famous mountains and landscapes dominated by lakes and rivers. Most northern mountains are large and high. The well-known mountainous topographical landscapes include: the Mt. Changbaishan of Jilin, the Mt. Qianshan and Benxi Water Caves of Liaoning, Mt. Taishan and Mt. Laoshan in Shandong, the Mt. Jigongshan and Mt. Songshan of Henan, Mt. Wutai, Mt. Hengshan and Mt. Wulaoshan in Shanxi, Mt. Huashan and Mt. Lishan of Shaanxi, and Mt. Bada—the Thirteen Emperors' tombs of Beijing, the Mt. Yeshanpo and Mt. Cangyanshan in Hebei, and Mt. Panshan in Tianjin. The landscapes dominated by water include: Jingpo Lake and Wuda Lianchi in Heilongjiang, Songhua and Jingyue Lakes in Jilin, the Yalujiang River and Dalian Seashore—Lushunkou sightseeing area and Xingcheng Island of Liaoning, and the beaches of the Shandong Peninsula.

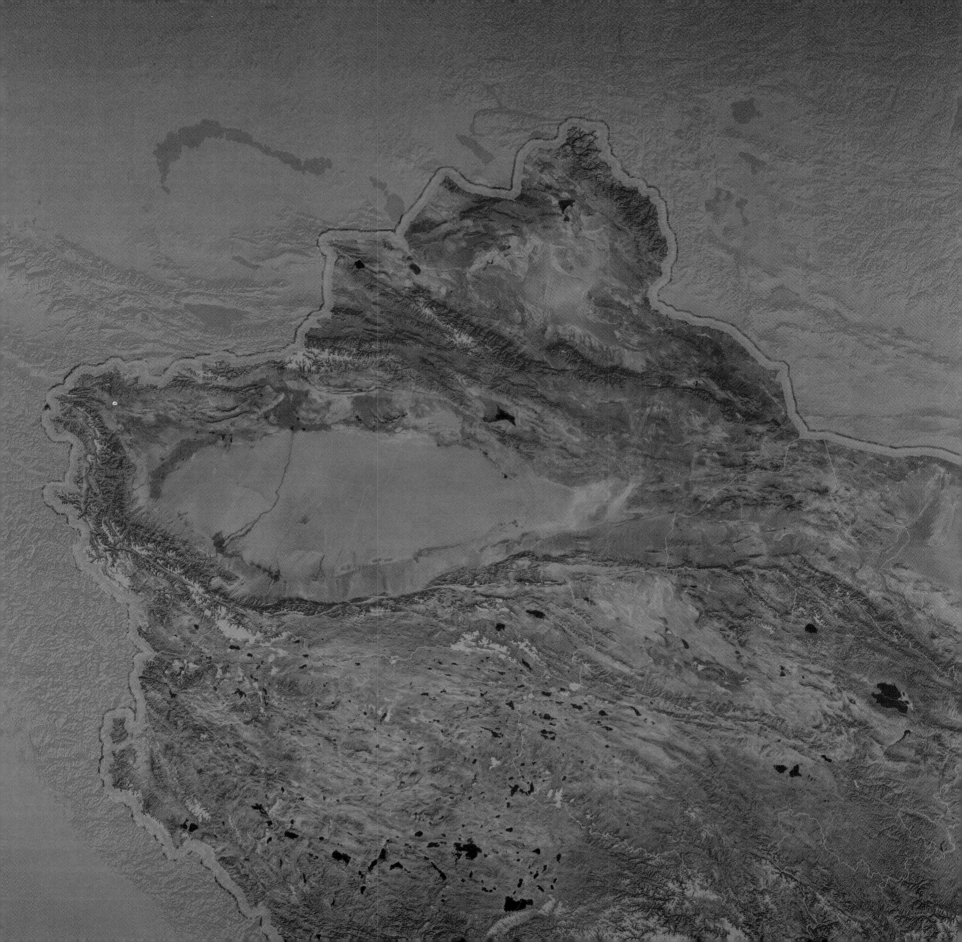

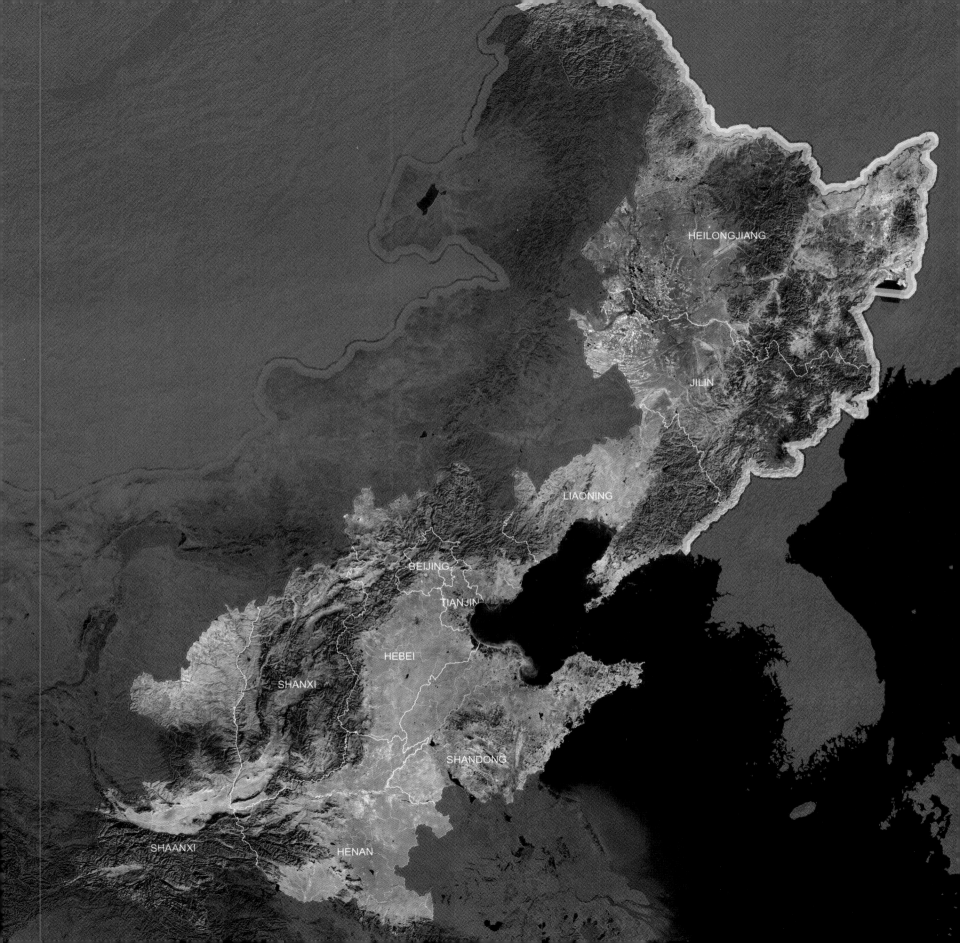

Birches in spring

A village of Heilongjiang Province in winter

Winter scene

Changbaishan Tianchi

Tianchi, in the shape of "oval" is the most famous landscape in Mt. Changbaishan, being the largest crater lake in China formed by volcanic eruption. It lies at an altitude of 2,150 meters, its deepest point being 204 meters.

The autumn scene in northeast China

Mt. Fenghuangling in Liaoning Province

**Bashang Landscape**

Bashang area is in the boundary between Hebei and Inner Mongolia, and is called Saihanba in Mongolian, meaning beautiful plateau. The grassy scene of Bashang in July is most charming.

Bashang Landscape
The rising sun shines on Bashang

Bashang Scenery

Baiyangdian Lake
Located in central Hebei Province, the Baiyangdian Lake Scenic Area is close to Baoding City. The lake,composed of many lakes of varied sizes, is famous for some 300 species of lotus flowers.

### Mt. Yuntai

Mt. Yuntai World Geological Park is in the south of Taihang Mountain in Xiuwu County. Its name originated from its high mountains and dangerous peaks wreathed in clouds.

### Mt. Huashan

Mt. Huashan, in Huayin of Shaanxi Province at an altitude of 2,200 meters, is a State-level scenic spot. The mountain offers a severe challenge for climbers with its many cliffs and crags.

### The Yellow River

The Yellow River plunges down at Hukou of Shanxi Province into the loess plateau. The river originates from the Qinghai-Tibet Plateau, meanders across Qinghai, Sichuan, Gansu, Loess Plateau, Ningxia, Inner Mongolia, Shaanxi and Shanxi and the Ordos Grassland, then into Henan and Shandong in the North China Plain, before emptying into the Bohai Gulf. It is 5,464 kilometers long, and drains a basin of 750,000 square kilometers.

 Hukou Fall

Hukou Fall in Shanxi is the largest along the watercourse of the Yellow River bestriding Shaanxi and Shanxi provinces. The water plunges down with a great sound, echoing off the cliffs and crags on the banks. Viewed from below, the water looks as if it is pouring from the sky.

Laoniuwan on the Yellow River

Laoniuwan is one of the 99 bays along the Yellow River. It is located in Pianguan of Shanxi Province. Here, the protuberant riverbank is like an ox tongue.with part of the Great Wall protecting the Yellow River for thousands of years. The guard tower in the picture is the only one along the Great Wall extending into the Yellow River, named Wanghelou.

The Great Wall
The Great Wall in China is the most lasting and largest national defensive works in world history, and a wonder of the world created by the ancient people of China. It stretches many thousands of miles.

# Southern Area

The southern area covers six provinces: Jiangsu, Zhejiang, Anhui, Jiangxi, Hunan and Hubei as well as Shanghai Municipality mid and downstream of the Yangtze River; the three provinces of Sichuan, Yunnan and Guizhou and Chongqing Municipality in the southwestern region; the four provinces of Guangdong, Fujian, Hainan and Taiwan; Guangxi Zhuang Autonomous Region; and two special administration regions of Hong Kong and Macao.

The climate, natural landscape and way of life of the southern area are markedly different from that of the northern area. In the eastern half of China, The "Mt. Qinlingshan-Huaihe River" is an important geological line that separates the north from the south. To the south of the line are found subtropical and tropical climatic zones of low elevation with annual precipitation of more than 800 mm. Temperature becomes warmer and warmer as one moves southward. There are no icy rivers in winter as in the north. Large rivers and lakes can be found everywhere. They make for some beautiful and elaborate natural scenery and landscapes.

In areas mid and downstream of the Yangtze River, the terrain is flat with crisscrossing rivers and widely scattered lakes. The five largest freshwater lakes of China—Poyanghu Lake, Dongtinghu Lake, Taihu Lake, Hongzehu Lake and Chaohu Lake—are all to be found here. The land surrounding the lakes is often dominated by rich, low-lying plains.

The southwestern part of the southern area comprises the Sichuan Basin and the Yunnan-Guizhou Plateau, which boasts a dizzying variety of topographies. The Sichuan Basin is surrounded by plateaus and mountains. Many high mountains are located on the Yunnan-Guizhou Plateau. Many of China's largest karst formations are found in the southwest, forming weird and wonderful scenes of stone forests, peaks and caves. The area is home to many extremely rare animals and plants. Pandas, the great symbol of China, are mostly found here. Xishuangbanna, located in southwest Yunnan, where it is hot and rainy all year round, is famous for its mountainous tropical forest. It is one of only two typical tropical landscapes in China, the other being on Hainan Island.

The southeastern part of the southern area includes the five provinces of Guangdong, Guangxi, Fujian, Hainan and Taiwan as well as Hong Kong and Macao. Most of the climate of the area is tropical, which gives rise to characteristic tropical scenery, evergreen trees, multitudinous flowers blooming all year round and fresh fruits blossoming each month. The Pearl River is the largest river in this region. Its major tributary, the Lijiang River, also known as the Guijiang River, is flanked by wondrous karst peaks. On both sides are found green mountains abounding in flourishing bamboo, through which run many clear rivers. The scenery here is world famous. As one of China's most well known sightseeing spots, the area attracts millions of tourists from all around the world each year. Many foreign visitors prove reluctant to leave after viewing this scenery and some choose to relocate here to live and work beside the Lijiang River.

The southern area is home to extensive ranges of hills. The Jiangnan Hills join up with the hills in the southeastern region. They are collectively known as the Southeastern Hills. The southern area is characterized by wondrous scenery and lots of famous mountains, many of which, although not especially high, are nevertheless magnificent to behold. Mt. Huangshan is famous all over China. Its peculiar pines, strange stone formations, hot springs and Cloud Sea form four distinct attractions. Some of the coral reef terrain, abrasion geomorphy and basalt rock formations found in Taiwan are absolutely unique.

The famous mountainous landscapes of the south include: Mt. Yuntaishan in Jiangsu, Mt. Yandangshan, Mt. Putuoshan and Mt. Tiantaishan in Zhejiang, Mt. Huangshan, Mt. Jiuhuashan and Mt. Langyashan in Anhui, Mt. Lushan, Mt. Sanqingshan and Mt. Jinggangshan in Jiangxi, Mt. Hengshan and Mt. Wulingyuan in Hunan, Mt. Wudangshan in Hubei, Mt. Emeishan and Mt. Huanglongshan-Jiuzaigou and Mt. Qingchengshan in Sichuan, the Forest stones, Yulong Snow Mountain and Xishuangbanna in Yunnan, the Zhijin Caves in Guizhou, Mt.Danxiashan and Mt. Xiqiaoshan in Guangdong, Mt. Wuyishan and Mt. Tailaoshan in Fujian, and Mt. Alishan in Taiwan. The major water landscapes include: Taihu Lake and Shugang-the Thin West Lake of Jiangsu, the West Lake and the Fuchunjiang River-Xin'anjiang River (Thousand Island Lake) in Zhejiang, Dian Lake, "Three Rivers Merging into One"and Ruilijiang River in Yunnan, the Huangguoshu Falls, Yuanjiang River and Hongfeng Lake in Guizhou, the Yangtze River Three Gorges in Chongqing, the Sun-Moon Pool in Taiwan, the tropical scenery of Hainan and many offshore islands.

Yunnan and Guangxi are the two most beautiful places in China, where endless spectacular scenery can be seen. Taiwan and Hainan are the two biggest islands in China. High mountains and low plains can both be found on these islands. The topography is characterized by startlingly unique scenery.

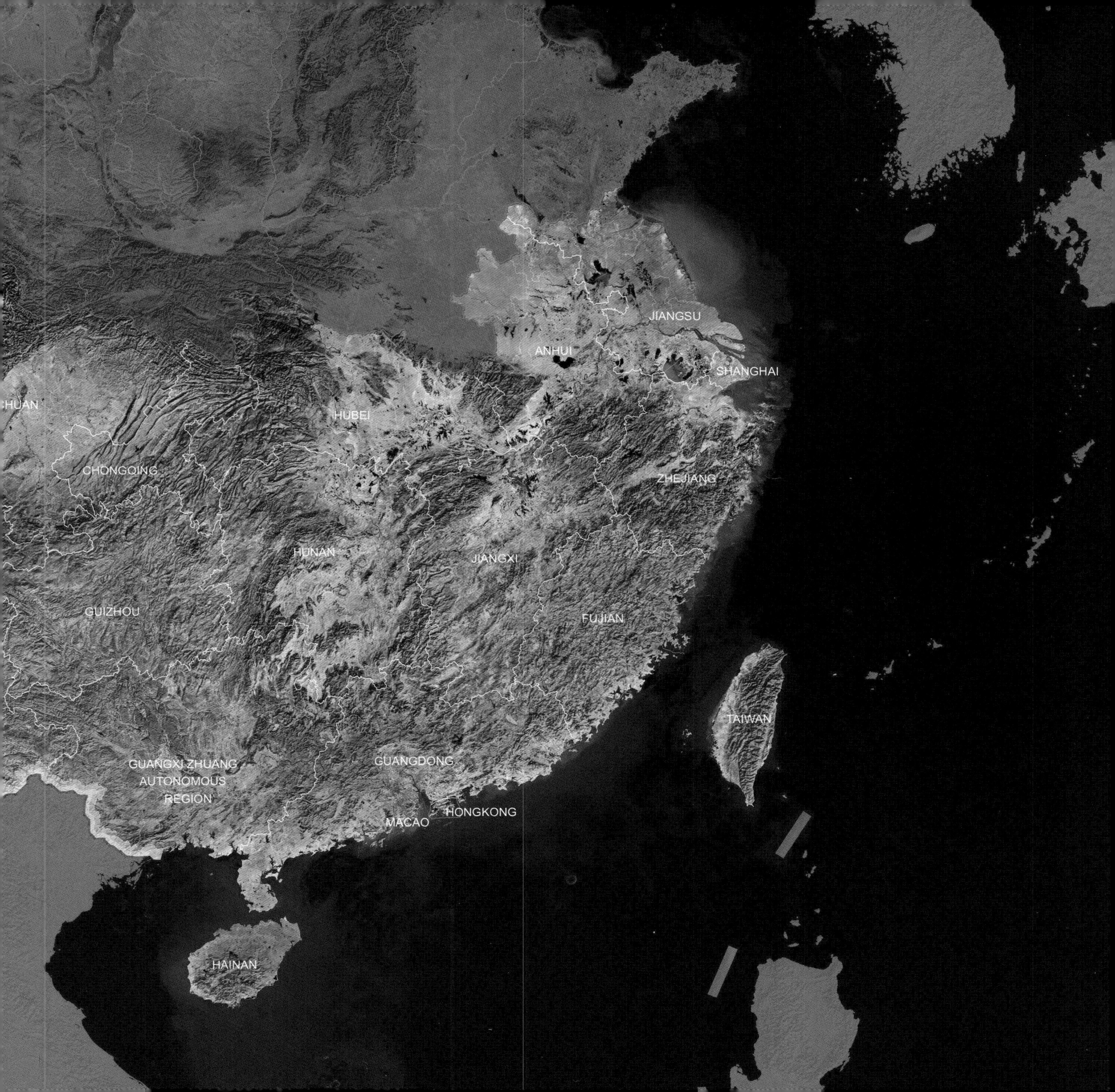

JIANGSU
ANHUI
SHANGHAI
CHUAN
HUBEI
CHONGQING
ZHEJIANG
HUNAN
JIANGXI
GUIZHOU
FUJIAN
TAIWAN
GUANGXI ZHUANG
AUTONOMOUS
REGION
GUANGDONG
HONGKONG
MACAO
HAINAN

Qiandaohu Lake

Qiandaohu ( Thousand Island ) Lake lies to the west of Hangzhou, Zhejiang Province. It is a man-made lake formed by damming during construction of the Xinanjiang River Power Station in 1959. It is dotted with numerous islands, while the towering hills around are reflected in the clear water.

### West Lake

West Lake in Hangzhou and surrounding hills set each other off in shining brilliance. The hills around the West Lake are no more than 400 meters high, but still look most impressive; the wooded slopes are quiet and beautiful clustering around West Lake like stars surrounding the moon.

Fangyan National Park of Yongkang, Zhejiang Province

**Mt. Huangshan**

Mt. Huangshan in southern Anhui Province is on the World Natural Heritage List. It is formed by a series of hills, and is especially famous for "ts beautiful pine trees, jagged rocks in strange shapes, rapidly changing clouds and bubbling hot springs".

### Mt. Sanqingshan

Mt. Sanqingshan forms part of the Huaiyu Mountain Range in the northeast of Shangrao,jiangxi Province. The altitude of its highest peak,Yujing,is 1,816.9 meters. Each side of the mountain reflects a totally different facet and character. The view is beautiful and elegant all around the year. It is a State-level scenic resort and historic spot.

## Mt. Lushan

Mt. Lushan in Jiangxi Province provides a pleasing contrast of rivers, lakes, sloping fields and hills. Dahanyang Peak is the highest at 1,474 meters. It is dotted with numerous ridges, gullies, and jagged rocks. The waters cascading off the sides eventually flow into paddy fields at the bottom. The famous Three-Step Spring falls through about 155 meters.

### Zhangjiajie

Zhangjiajie is the most famous landscape in Mt. Wulingshan situated in the north of Dayong, Hunan Province. Its most characteristic features are its quartz sandstone landforms. Wulingyuan Scenic Area covers more than 40,000 square kilometers and is in the World Natural Heritage List.

Shennongjia in Hubei Province

Longlin Palace in Enshi

Longlin Palace is situated in the headstream of Kylin Brook in the western suburbs of Enshi City, Hubei Province, and comprises both water and dry caves, some as long as 2,300 meters.

**Daocheng Landscape**

Yading Nature Reserve in Daocheng is situated on the southwest border of Sichuan. The three divine mountains in Daocheng have been sacred places of Tibetan Buddhism since ancient times.

Mt. Gonggar

Located in Garze Tibetan Autonomous Prefecture of Sichuan, Mt. Gonggar means "the highest snow-covered mountain" in Tibetan.

**Huanglong**
Huanglong Scenic Area is located on the northern mountains of Sichuan. It joins with nearby Jiuzhaigou as two bright pearls included in the World Natural Heritage List. Huanglong was a complete glacier, about 30,000 years ago. The retreat of the glacier helped form the karst landscape of high mountains and colorful lakes of today.

## Mt. Emeishan

Mt. Emeishan is a famous Buddhism mountain, located in the southern suburbs of Emeishan City in the southwest Sichuan Basin. It includes four mountains. Mt. Emeishan's position is just like an eyebrow. There are more than 30 ancient temples, and every day the area resounds to morning bells and Buddhist chants. It is included in the World Cultural Heritage List.

Mt. Qingchengshan

Mt. Qingchengshan is in the northwest border of the Chengdu Plain, within Dujiangyan. Its highest peak, Laoxiaoding, is 1,600 meters above sea level. Being renowned as the "quietest spot in the world", it is one of the Taoism mountains.

**Nuorilang Fall in Jiuzhaigou**

Jiuzhaigou is located in Nanping County of Sichuan, its name originated from the nine Tibetan villages around it. It is a fairyland of snowy and lofty mountains, wooden buildings, waving flags, traditional customs and numerous legends. It is part of the Mingshan Mountain Range. Nuorilang Fall has a drop of 20 meters but a width of 300 meters.

### Leshan Giant Buddha

The Leshan Giant Buddha is found in the suburbs of Leshan, Sichuan Province, at the confluence of the Minjiang, Qingyihe and Daduhe rivers. The Giant Buddha, 71 meters high and with an instep width of 8.5 meters was chiseled in the crag of Qixia Peak of Mt. Lingyun.

Heilong pool

Heilong pool, also called Yuquan Park, is located at the foot of Mt Xiangshan in Lijiang, Yunnan Province. Numerous springs flow out from the foot of the mountain,and make a pool covering thousands of square meters .The natural scenery and the architecrure of the Ming and Qing Dynasties (1368-1911)complement each other.

Mt. Danxiashan

Paddy Fields in Zhanyi

Zhanyi County is located in Yunnan, and it is also the cradle of the Pearl River. Here, the horse tassel flowers are lovely while the lakes are clear. The Niulan River Canyon is also a place of great charm.

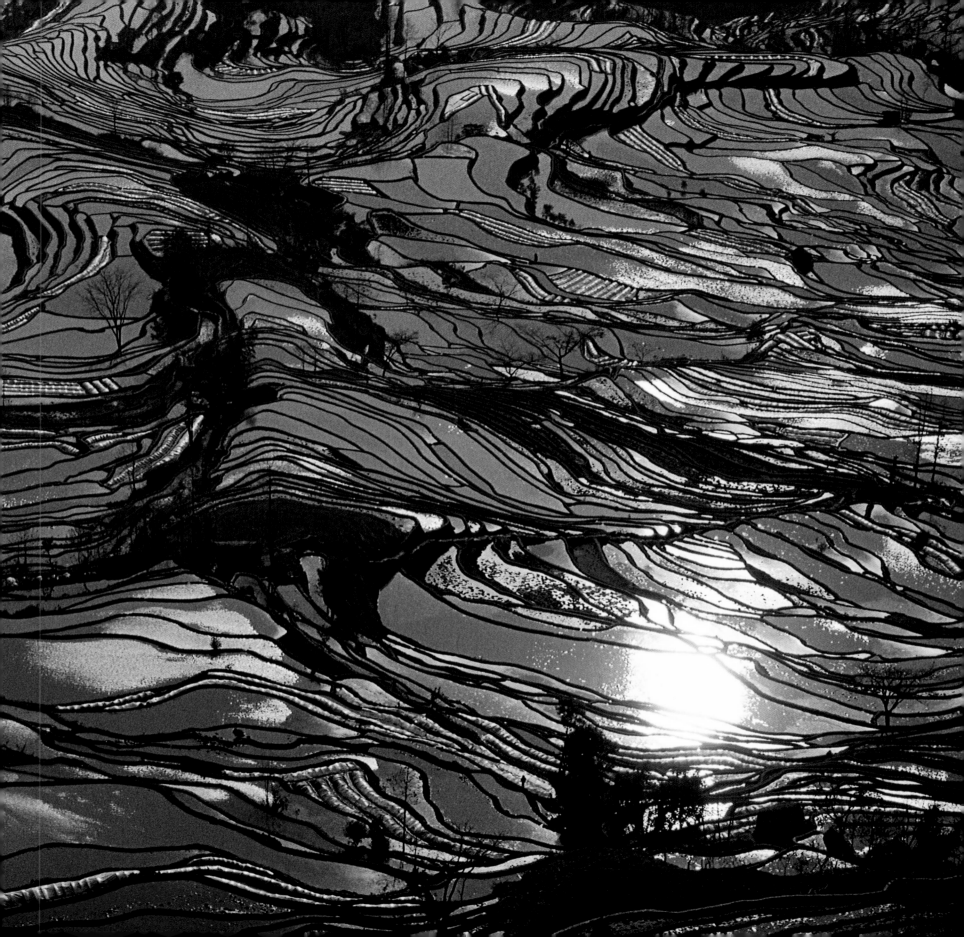

Lugu Lake in Yunnan Province

◁ Yuanyang Terrace

The Yuanyang Terrace is located in Yuanyang County, Honghe Prefecture in Yunnan. It is the core of the Hani Terrace in Honghe, covering about 20,000 square kilometers, and is situated between hills with an elevation ranging from 200 to 2,000 meters and with a gradient of about 25 degrees.

### The First Bay of the Yangtze River

The First Bay of the Yangtze River is located in Shigu of Lijiang, Yunnan Province. The section of the river running through Yunnan is called the Jinshajiang River. In the low water period (April and May), sandbanks appear, and there are beautiful paddy fields along the riverside.

Huangguoshu Fall
Among the many scenic spots and historical sites of Huangguoshu, located in southwest Guizhou, there is a large waterfall with a height of 74 meters, and a width of 81 meters.

Seaside of Zhanjiang in Guangdong

## U-Turn of Jinshajiang River

In Derong, Yunnan province, the Jinshajiang River makes a great u-turn around the almost Perfetly tapered mountain of Derong. The river is a section of the upper Yandtze River between palthang in Yushu the upper Yangtze River between Palthang in Yushu County, Qinghai province and the Minjiang River in Yibin, SIchuan Province.

◁ Detian Fall

The Detian Fall is near the frontier between China and Vietnam. The Guichun River divides into two here, the mainstream in China forming Detian Fall of 120 meters wide; the other branch in Vietnam forms the Banyue Fall. Together, they form one of the largest waterfall systems in Asia.

Lijiang River

Mt. Wuyishan
Mt. Wuyishan, located in the southern
suburbs of Wuyishan City, Fujian Province,
is composed of colorful breccia, and
belongs to the Danxia landform.

Jinhu Scenic Area, Fujian Province

### Sun-Moon Pool

Sun-Moon Pool is located in Nantou County in the center of Taiwan Province. Guanghua Island divides the pool into two parts, which are just like the arc of moon and the wheel of the sun respectively, so it is called "Sun-Moon Pool", Amid piled-up hills, the wide lake with clear water reflects all the seasonal changes.

Tianyahaijiao

Tianyahaijiao, located in Sanya City of Hainan Province, is a famous scenic spot.  The coconut trees and sail shadows are so charming and gentle.

### Snow Scene in Mt. Yushan

Yushan Park is located in the center of Taiwan Province at an altitude of 3,950 meters. With the Yushan hills in the center, it faces Taidong coastal mountain range in the east, and the Mt. Alishan in the west. It is a typical sub-tropical park in a high mountain area.

**Wuxia Gorge**

The Three Gorges from Yichang of Hubei Province to Chaotianmen Dock of Chongqing City are a renowned scenic resort and historic spot. The mountains, valleys and natural zoology protection region combine with historic human scenes in an organic way that is the most attractive.

Yangtze River Three Gorges
The gorges constitute the most famous scenic area of China. It stretches from Baidi City in Fengjie
County of Chongqing in the west to Nanjinguan in Yichang City of Hubei Province. It is a cradle of the
ancient civilization of China.

# Northwestern Area

The northwest area consists of Gansu Province and the Inner Mongolia autonomous region, Ningxia Hui autonomous region and Xinjiang Uygur autonomous region. These are areas where there is very little annual precipitation; rivers are not plentiful and tend to be mostly inland rivers. Consequently vegetation and human population is also very much less in this vast area than in other areas of China. Topographically speaking, the northwest area consists mainly of plateaus and basins. The Inner Mongolian Plateau (1,000-1,500 meters above sea level), contains a lot of hilly territory with low land between the hills. The Hexi Corridor, west of the Inner Mongolian Plateau, is a narrow valley formed by several basins, about 1,000 meters above sea level. The Tarim and Dzungarian Basins in Xinjiang are the two largest basins in China. The Turpan Basin is the lowest point in China. In the plateaus and basins are located large desert areas accounting for nearly 50 percent of China's total desert area. Major deserts include the Taklimakan Desert, the Gorban Tongot Desert in Xinjiang (second largest in China), the Badanchilin Desert, the Tengri Desert (Inner Mongolia), and the Kormotag Desert between Xinjiang and Gansu. The Taklimakan Desert is the largest desert both in China and in the world. It is located in the Tarim Basin in the south of Xinjiang. Most of its vast area consists of large sand hills and dunes. These sand hills are famous for their stunning variety of shapes. The desert supports almost no life due to the severity of its climate. The Gorban Tongot Desert is the second largest desert in China by area. It is located in the Dzungarian Basin, north of Xinjiang. Its climate is somewhat less harsh than that of the Taklimakan Desert. Thus some hardy trees manage to find enough sustenance to survive and grow here. The deserts of Inner Mongolia are favored by slightly more precipitation each year than the deserts further west. Some plants grow in the sand. Shrubbery can be found in low-lying ground among the sand hills. There are particular places where water accumulates—desert oases—which provide a literally life-giving water source for desert herdsmen, not to mention constituting one of the desert's most beautiful sights. Desert poplar trees grow tall and straight here, framing a beautiful green landscape in the very center of the barrenness of the desert.

Besides large areas of desert, the northwestern region also includes vast grassland territories. The grasslands of Inner Mongolia are extremely large in area—they constitute about one-third of the total grassland area of China. These pastures are of good quality. The lush grass of the vast grassland is like a green ocean. An ancient Chinese poem describes it thus: "Under the endless sky lies the endless grassland; the wind bends the grass to reveal sheep and cattle." This is indeed an emblematic evocation of the splendor of the Inner Mongolian grassland.

Mt. Tianshan, Mt. Kunlunshan and Mt. Altay in Xinjiang are all at least 2,000 meters above sea level. These towering mountains block the damp air stream, so a lot of precipitation falls on the high mountain slopes of the northwestern area. Flowers and fruits grow in great profusion in the green belts on both sides of Tianshan Mountain and the green belt to the south of Mt. Kunlunshan. There are also many fine pastures to be found in Xinjiang.

The northwest area is also an important section of the "Silk Road" —an immeasurably important link between East and West in ancient times.

The northwest area is also famed for the beauty of much of its natural scenery. Prominent mountains include: Mt. Maijishan and Mt. Kongtongshan in Gansu, the Greater Hing'an Mountain in Inner Mongolia, Mt. Helanshan in Ningxia, and Mt. Tianshan and Mt. Altay in Xinjiang. Lake and river beauty spots include the Yueya spring in Gansu, Shahu Lake in Ningxia, and Tianchi, Karnas and Marnas Lakes in Xinjiang. The area is also world famous for the breathtaking majesty of its desert and grassland landscapes.

XINJIANG UYGUR AUTONOMOUS REGION

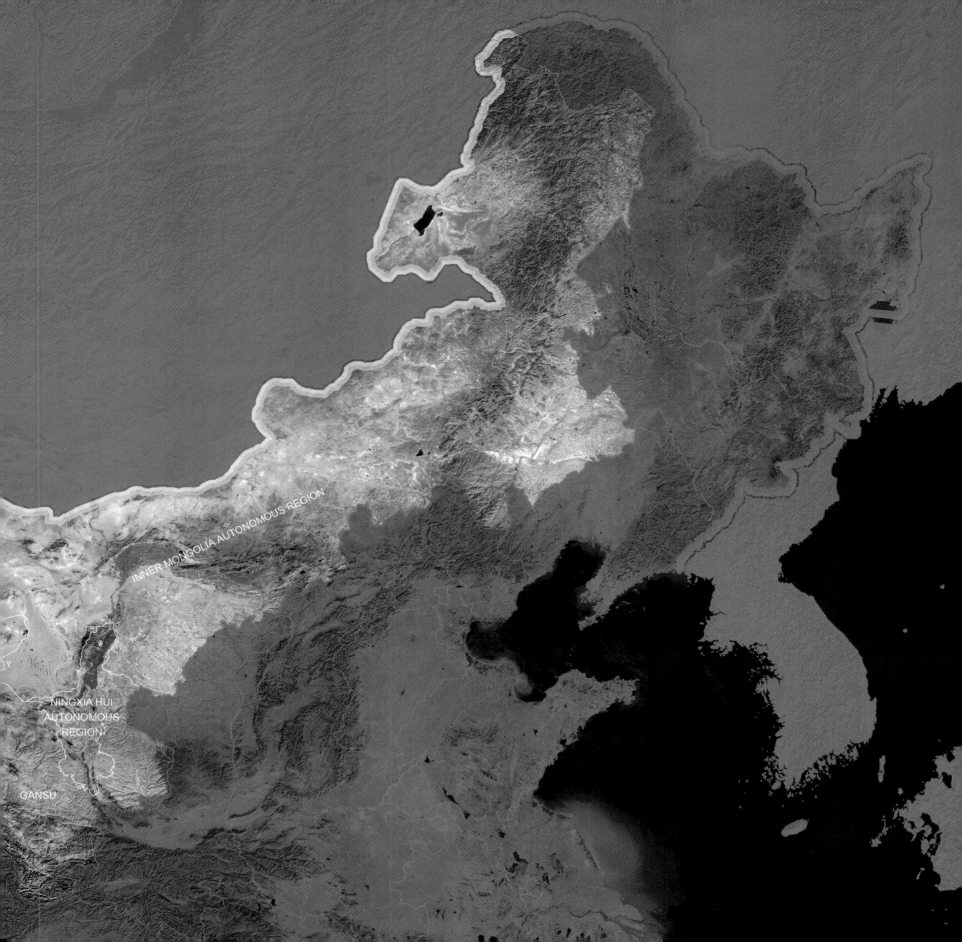

**Shandan Army Horse Ranch**
Shandan Army Horse Ranch is located in Qilianshan Horse Ranch in the south of Shandan County in the Zhangye area of Gansu Province. It is flat with plentiful water and grass, covered in greenery in summer and goldenness in winter. It is the biggest in Asia and the second largest in the world.

Loess Plateau Landform in Dingxi, Gansu Province

The Loess Plateau, north-central China, is one of the four prominent plateaus of China, and the largest loess sedimentary area in the world, covering around 400,000 square kilometers. It is where Chinese culture first emerged.

Loess Plateau Landform in Dingxi, Gansu Province

Wushaoling
Located in the central part of Tianzhu Tibetan Autonomous County of Gansu, Wushaoling refers to terraced fields featuring attractive scenery.

**Inner Mongolian Prairie**
Inner Mongolia has the most famous prairie in China. Verses, such as "Between the vast sky and the boundless earth, flocks and herds appear as grass bends to the wind",portray the essential nature of the area.

◁ Yadan Landform

The clay terrain there was eroded by rainstorms and baked by the sun intensively for thousands of years, and then formed the Yadan landform with all kinds of strange configurations.

Danxia Landform
Danxia Landform in Zhangye of Gansu features strange shapes and varied colors.

Keshiketeng Banner Stone Forest, Inner Mongolia

**Ergun River in Manchuria**

Ergun River is the original home of the Mongolians. It is a branch of the Heilongjiang River and forms with it the boundary between China and Russia.

Qilianshan—Hexi Corridor

Hexi Corridor is the long, narrow lowland between the Qilianshan and Beishan mountain ranges in Gansu. It contains a number of historically cultural cities such as Wuwei, Zhangye and Dunhuang. Travelers on the world-famous "Silk Road" started from here on their long journey to the West.

**Ejina Heicheng City Relic**
Ejina is the biggest Banner (administrative division) in Inner Mongolia. Located in the West, it has a boundless stretch of Gobi and vast bleak desert. The golden Huyang forest is the symbol of Ejina, being one of only three in the world. Heicheng in Ejina is the most complete ancient city existing along the ancient Silk Road.

Sand Whistling Bay
Located in Kubuchi Desert south of Baotou, Inner Mongolia, it is so named for the sound created by the movement of the sand dunes.

Mt. Xumishan
Located in the southeast of Yinchuan, Ningxia, the mountains form a severe barrier, with narrow gorges, deep ravines, dangerous gullies and towering peaks. The grottoes distributed among the eight cliffs are very famous.

Mausoleums of Western Xia Kings at Mt. Helanshan,Ningxia

**Wolong Bay**
Wolong Bay lies in the Hemo Karnas of the Mongolian rural area, almost 10 kilometers to Kenasi Lake in the north. It comprises a succession of zigzag rivers and bays. There is wide vision on the flat lawns on the east and west banks of the river.

Sunflowers in Inner Mongolia

Tarim River Huyang Trees

Tarim River Huyang Trees

**Tarim River Huyang Trees Nature Reserve**
The reserve lies between the Taklimakan Desert and the Kumutage Desert, and is the only original one of its kind in the world. Huyang, as "desert warrior", has very strong vitality, belonging to the genus of deciduous trees and having survived from the tertiary period.

"Eight Hundred Miles of Flame"
The locals use this description for Turpan Flaming Mountain in Xinjiang, which is composed of the Jura and chalk of the Mesozoic era and the red sand, conglomerate and mud from the tertiary period. A myriad of ravines score the mountain slopes. In summer, thermal air currents make it hard to breathe at times.

Rape flowers at the foot of Mt. Tianshan

Morning mist in Mt. Tianshan ▷

### Taklimakan Desert

Taklimakan Desert lies in the center of the Tarim Basin; it is the second largest desert in the world behind the Sahara in Africa. Its meaning is "entering without coming out" in the Uygur language and is also known as the "sea of death".

### Wucaicheng City

The city lies in Changji Hui Autonomous Prefecture in Xinjiang. It is a model of a Yadan physiognomy community. The rocks of the hills are reddish brown, mauve, grey green, orange, and desert tan. As they form shapes like a city skyline, the name of "wucaicheng (Five-Color Town)" emerged.

135

◁ Hemo Town
The town in Xinjiang is as beautiful as the ink-and-wash painting in winter.

Nalati Grassland
Nalati Grassland is located in Xinyuan County, Yili Kazak Autonomous Prefecture in Xinjiang. It has been a famous alpine meadow from ancient times.

**Sailimo Lake**
Sailimo Lake, located in the west of Mt. Tianshan, is the highest mountain lake with the biggest area in Xinjiang.

Tekesi Grassland

Tekesi Grassland in Tekesi County of Xinjiang has boundless flowers of rape, white snow-capped mountains and jade grasslands that combine to form a beautiful portrait.

141

Dzungarian Basin

### Tianchi Under Snow
Tianchi or the Heavenly Lake is located in Mt. Bogda of Mt. Tianshan in Fukang City. Xinjiang. It is very clear, with green grass on both sides. Trees blot out the sky and the sun while Mt. Bogda shines in the lake water.

**Mt. Bogda**

This lies in Fukang City of Xinjiang and is the highest peak in Tianshan. The peak is snow-capped and glaciers down the sides never melt even in summer. The clear water of the Tianchi in the valley creates a beautiful scene.

# Qinghai-Tibet Area

The Qinghai-Tibet area covers Qinghai Province and the Tibet Autonomous Region. Qinghai Province is located on the northeastern portion of the Qinghai-Tibet Plateau. It is the source of the Yangtze River, the Lancangjiang River and the Yellow River, and is understandably known as "the Source of all Rivers". Qinghai Lake is the largest saltwater lake in China. The Tsaidam Basin is located in the west of Qinghai and is commonly known as "the treasure basin". The Tibet Autonomous Region is located on the southwestern portion of the Qinghai-Tibet Plateau. It forms the main part of the plateau and is the principal area of inhabitation for people of the Tibetan ethnic group.

Originally, the Qinghai-Tibet Plateau was an ocean. About 2 million years ago, the Qinghai-Tibet Plateau had not yet been formed. It was many millennia later, after several large-scale movements of the earth's crust that it rose up and became the plateau with the largest area and the highest elevation in the world. Today, the Qinghai-Tibet Plateau is still an area where movements of the earth's crust are frequent. The total area of the Qinghai-Tibet Plateau is some 2.5 million square kilometers, accounting for a full one-fourth of the total continental area of China. With an average elevation of above 4,000 meters, it is also called the "Roof of the World".

The Qinghai-Tibet Plateau is a veritable sea of mountains, especially high mountains. About 50 high peaks here each exceed 7,000 meters in height, and 11 others are over 8,000 meters high.

The peaks over 5,000 meters above sea level are covered with snow all year round, and many large mountainous glaciers have been formed. The Himalayas is the world highest and youngest mountain range. The range extends for more than 2,400 kilometers from Kashmir to Namgabawa Peak, with an average elevation of over 6,000 meters. Mt. Qomolangma, which has the shape of a large pyramid and is located on the border between China and Nepal, is the main peak of the range. It is 8,848 meters high and is the highest mountain in the world. Around the peak are found a number of glaciers of various sizes and shapes. These glaciers too are a stunning sight. These natural ice sculptures were created by sunshine. Generally, this phenomenon takes dozens of years. The ice towers on Mt.Qomolangma and in the Shishabangma Peak areas are the most wonderful of the world's continental glaciers.

The Yarlung Zangbo River, which is held as a "mother river" by Tibetans, is the longest river in Tibet. It runs across the south of the Qinghai-Tibet Plateau and is joined by many tributary rivers, forming a river so wide and powerful that broad valleys are cut through the mountains by its force. Approaching the boundary between Mainling and Medog Counties in eastern Tibet, the river is blocked by the enormous Mt. Namjagbarwa, the highest peak in the eastern Himalayas. Here the river carves out a peculiar "U" shaped gorge. This gorge is of much greater dimensions than others of its kind both in terms of length and depth.

There are many famous lakes in the Qinghai-Tibet area. Most of them are inland lakes created by snow-melt water flowing down from high mountain slopes to more low lying areas. Nam Co in northern Tibet is the largest lake in Tibet and is famed for its crystal clear blue water and majestic scenery. The highest freshwater lake in the world is Lake Mapang Yumco, widely regarded as a holy lake, in the Ali area of Tibet.

The grasslands of northern Tibet cover an area of some 400,000 square kilometers. They form one of the five largest pasture areas in China. In ancient times, the area was called "Changtang". This vast and relatively unpopulated region is a paradise for wild animals.

Kukushiri is the largest area completely without human habitation on the Qinghai-Tibet Plateau and is dotted with unique landscapes. The valleys of southern Tibet are furnished with large forested areas, which girdle the lower mountain slopes. Lake Qinghai, which is located in the northeast of Qinghai and is surrounded by mountains, covers an enormous area. The birds' island in the lake is a paradise for many thousands of birds. The Hengduan mountainous region and "Three Parallel Rivers" in the east of the Qinghai-Tibet Plateau are also home to a multitude of fascinating landscapes.

The most famous mountains in the Qinghai-Tibet Region are: Mt. Qomolangma, Gangrinpoche Peak, Lhoze Peak, Namjagbarwa Peak, Shishabangma Peak, which are all in Tibet, and the Mt. Kunlunshan and Mt. Riyueshan in Qinghai. The major landscapes dominated by water include the Nam Co, Serlign Co, Basum Co, Yamzhog Yumco, Mawang Yutso, Ra'g Co and Panggong Tso Lakes, and the Yarlung River Valley in Tibet and Qinghai Lake and the Three-River (the Yangtze, Yellow and Lancangjiang Rivers) Nature Reserve in Qinghai.

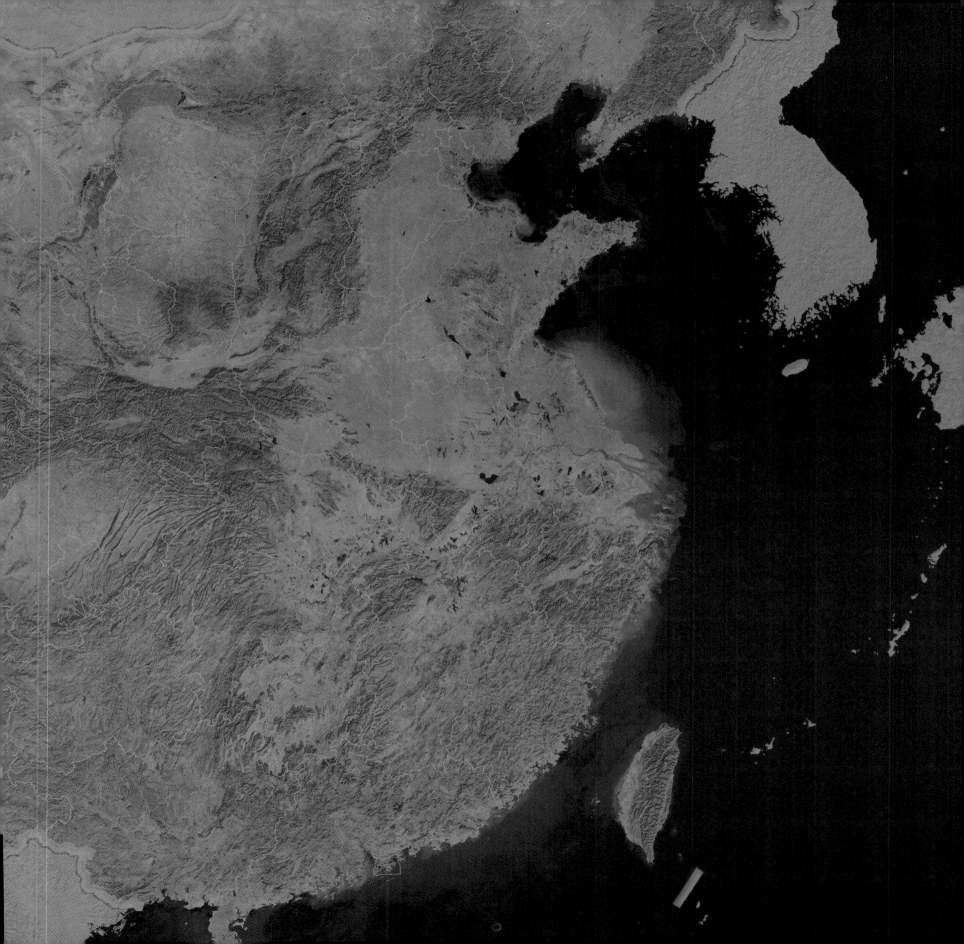

Rural area of Huangnan in Qinghai

### Geladandong Glacier

Geladandong Glacier in Qinghai is the highest peak in the Tanggula Mountain Range. The Jianggendiru Glacier in the south is the origin of Tuotuo River, namely the source of the Yangtze River. The serac forest, ice bridge, ice lake, and ice stalactites form a unique ice-carved world.

Qinghai Lake Bird Island

Qinghai Lake, located in the northeast of the Qinghai-Tibet Plateau, is the biggest inland saltwater lake in China. Qinghai Lake Bird Island is a focal point for birds; there are tens of thousands of birds coming from all over the world to breed or rest every year.

155

◁ Kukushiri Wild Ass

Kukushiri Zoological Nature Reserve lies in the northwest of Qinghai, forming the hinterland of the Qinghai-Tibet Plateau, and lying at an attitude above 4,600 meters. The no-man area is a haven for wild animals; although the species are limited, many are almost unique to the Qinghai-Tibet Plateau. The Tibet wild ass, looks like a cross between an ass and a horse, and with a tail like the latter has earned the name of "wild horse".

158

### Kukushiri Wild Yak

The wild yak is the biggest vegetarian animal in the plateau, the obvious difference between a wild yak and a domesticated one is that, the former has long, black, and brown down all over its body and it is rather huge in stature.

Morning in the Himalayas, Burang

Burang County in Ngari Prefecture of Tibet is the southwestern door of the Qinghai-Tibet Plateau, with the Himalayas in the south, and Gangdise in the north. The Himalayas form a great arc running east-west for 2,450 kilometers, with more than 50 separate mountains each higher than 7,000 meters.

### Qomolangma

Qomolangma lies in the middle of the Himalayas serving as the boundary of China and Nepal, and with a height of 8,848 meters. Within a scope of 20 kilometers there stand so many towering peaks and mountain ranges.

**Qomolangma Glaciers**
There are glaciers and serac forests of varying sizes and shapes in the mountain area around Qomolangma. These form a beautiful world of ice carvings.

◁ Holy Mountain Phari in Tibet

Nyingchi in summer, Tibet

Big Bend of the Yarlung Zangbo

On the border between Mainling County and Medog County, the Yarlung Zangbo is forced to change direction and forms a big U-shaped turn.

Clay Forest in Zada
Clay Forest lies in Zada County of Ngari. The banks of Xiangquanhe River in Zada are encircled by loess hillocks meandering on for many miles, with the bleak and solemn beauty. The special physiognomy formed by water erosion is similar as that in the Western United States.

Holy Lake of Dochen Co
Lakes and wetlands constitute the unique ecological system in the Qinghai-Tibet Plateau. They retain water and protect diversified forms of ecological environment.

**Daerguo Holy Mountain**
The mountains of the Qinghai-Tibet Plateau all have religious connotations. Daerguo Holy Mountain lies in Bangoin County in northern Tibet and is revered by adherents of Tibetan Buddhism and the Tibetan Bon religion.

**Mt. Shishabangma**
Mt. Shishabangma is the sole peak with an altitude of more than 8,000 meters completely in China; it is about 120 kilometers from Qomolangma in the southeast. There is a valley glacier with numerous icy towers, about 10 kilometers long on its northern slope.

Highway zigzags through the Himalayas

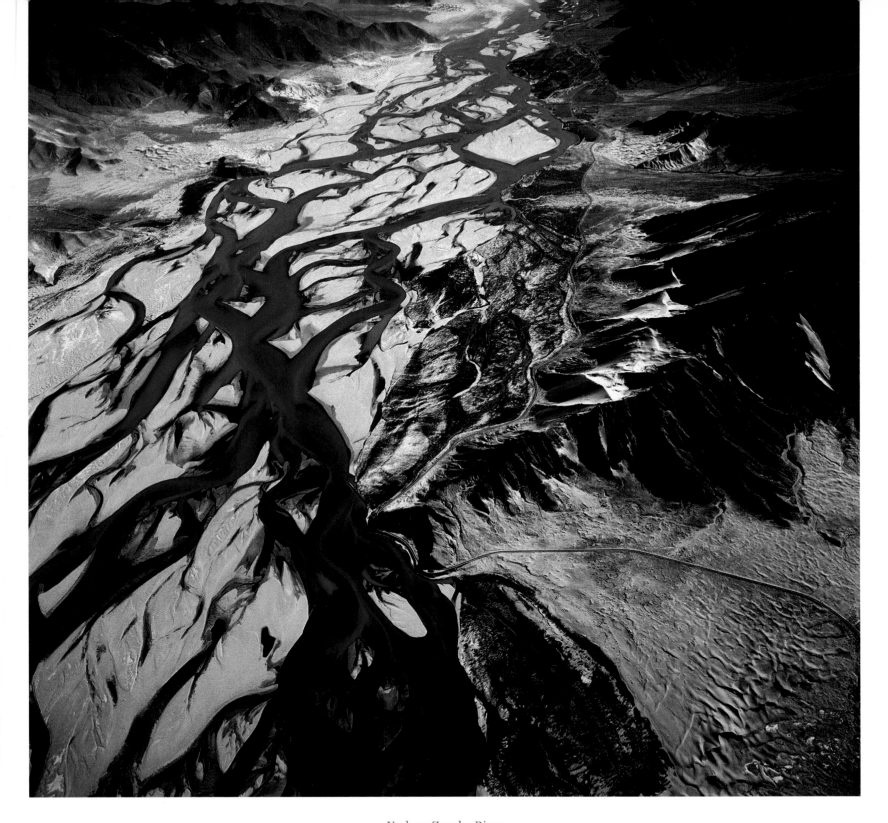

**Yarlung Zangbo River**

The Yarlung Zangbo River flows south from the Qinghai-Tibet Plateau and is an international water system with a drainage area of 935,000 square kilometers. The scenery along the banks is very beautiful.

Holy Lake of Nam Co

Nam Co lies between Bangoin County and Damxung County, and is the largest lake in Tibet, and the highest lake in the world. It has abundant water and grass, so it is the best natural meadow in northern Tibet. It has particular karst landforms in its central island. In the Tibetan Year of the Sheep, Tibetans will walk around Nam Co clockwise on a pilgrimage.

Holy Mountain Gangrinpoche, in Tibet

### Ra'og Co and Ancient Glaciers

Ra'og Co is located in Baxoi County of Qamdo Prefecture, and it was formed by mud-rock flows. It is a large lake at high altitude. Gangrigabu snow peak lies to the southwest and Azhagongla Glacier to the south. The scenery of green meadow, pure blue lake and white snow peaks is beautiful.

**Pangong Lake in Ngari**
Pangong means "an enchanting, long and narrow lake" in Tibetan, lying at an altitude of 4,242 meters, it is a key lake on the Qinghai-Tibet Plateau and a haven for birds.

Ra'og Co

Ra'og Co is a bright pearl inlaid in the border between Sichuan and Tibet, with the snowy mountains, blue lake and Tibetan villages creating a harmonious picture between nature and human beings.

# ‖ Photographers

Bian Zhiwu

Chang Ning

Du Zequan

Jiang Ping

Luo Hong

Li Shaobai

Li Xueliang

Song Jupu

Shi Lei

Sun Qunli

Shi Yongting

Wang Jin

Wu Jian

Wang Dequan

Wang Junwu

Xiao Dianchang

Xu Zhaopang

Yang Bingzheng

Yuan Xuejun

Yu Yuntian

Zhang Chaoyin

Zheng Yunfeng

China Foto Press

Beijing Quanjing Scientific and Technological Co., Ltd

Map Artwork: Huang Qian    Design: Zhang Yajing

图书在版编目（CIP）数据

中国风光／林武汉主编；王国振译．—北京：五洲传播
出版社，2008.4
ISBN 978-7-5085-1276-1

．Ⅰ.中… Ⅱ.①林…②王… Ⅲ.风光摄影—中国
—现代—摄影集 Ⅳ．J424

中国版本图书馆CIP数据核字（2008）第129423号


顾　　问：杨逸畴
主　　编：林武汉
执行主编：张超音
策　　划：荆孝敏
责任编辑：荆孝敏　张美景


出版发行：五洲传播出版社
　　　　　社址：北京市海淀区北小马厂6号
　　　　　邮政编码：100038
　　　　　电话：58891281
　　　　　传真：58891281
印　　刷：北京画中画印刷有限公司
开　　本：1/12
印　　张：16
版　　次：2008年6月第2版
印　　次：2009年12月第2次印刷
书　　号：ISBN 978-7-5085-1276-1
定　　价：220.00元